Dolphins : A Kids Book About These Cool Creatures in the Sea.

Terry Mason

What is a Dolphin?

Dolphins are marine mammals, which means that though they live in the oceans and rivers they are warm blooded and give live birth, unlike your average fish who is cold blooded and lay eggs.

Dolphins are considered one of the smartest marine animals and are well known for their acrobatic ability. Their natural abilities and intelligence is one reason they are a very popular marine animal for public attractions.

Types of Dolphins

There are 33 types of dolphins and they can be found in waterways all around the world. In addition to the basic dolphin there are also 4 types of river dolphins, 6 types of porpoise. Dolphins range in size from a mere 4 foot long and 90 pounds to 30 foot long and 10 tons. Some of the most well-known dolphins include:

Baby-pink river dolphin

Bottlenose Dolphin

Striped Dolphin

Atlantic Spotted Dolpin

Dusky Dolphin

Mahi-Mahi-Or-DolphinOrca dolphin

It may surprise you to learn that the killer whale and orca are also a part of the dolphin family.

Dolphin Body

Dolphin appearance will vary among the different types, but most have the same basic body construction.

•**Beak**- dolphins have a beak rather than a nose with the exception of porpoises and killer wales or orcas, who have a flat square jaw rather than a long beak.

•**Dorsal fin**- all dolphins have a dorsal fin, though some types have a barely noticeable ridge rather than a full blown fin. This fin provides balance and stability.

•**Flukes**- what you might refer to as a tail are actually called flukes, each dolphin has two of them and they help propel them through the water.

•**Blowhole**- all dolphins have a blow hole which is where they get air and discharge sound. Unlike us a dolphin must consciously breathe, when means they have to tell their body to take a breath. Very useful when you spend a lot of time underwater.

•**Flipper**- as you know dolphins do not have hands, instead they have flippers or pectoral fins. Interestingly inside the pec fins are bone structures similar to the human hand and arm bones. These fins help control direction when swimming.

Dolphin Habitats

If you want to see a dolphin in the wild there are several places you can go. In the United States the Florida coastal regions are popular for dolphin watching.

As a rule dolphins prefer warm shallow waters, though the bottlenose has been known to travel to colder climates in pursuit of food.

All but a few dolphin types live in saltwater, but a couple actually thrive in fresh water.

Some dolphins follow a set migration path, travelling hundreds of miles every year in pursuit of food and still others will change course during migration depending on the food supply.

What Do Dolphins Eat?

Dolphin-Eats-Fresh-Fish

Fish is the main item on the dolphin menu. Usually herring, cod and mackerel are the preferred dinner time selection, but this will vary depending on the type of dolphin.

As you might imagine bigger dolphins such as the Killer Whale will eat seals, turtles and sea lions in addition to varying types of fish.

What is really interesting is the way some types of dolphins hunt for food. Several dolphins will work together to herd a school of fish, they will swim around and around the school packing them in tightly and then different members will dive through the fish eating their fill in the process.

Dolphin diets include:

•Mackerel

•Herring

•Cod

•Squid

•Turtles

In addition to herding dolphins will also stun prey with their tales, corral them in shallow areas or even beach or strand fish to eat at their leisure.

Dolphin Communication

Dolphins make a broad range of sounds which are created by the air sacs beneath the blow hole. Dolphin sounds fall into three basic categories, whistles, clicks and burst pulse vocalizations. These sounds serve several purposes including but not limited to:

•**Echolocation**- dolphin clicks are thought to be a locating mechanism, as a dolphin gets closer to an item of interest the clicks will get longer and more frequent. Echolocation allows animals to determine distance from the echoes produced when sound hits a solid object. Bats have the same type of location system.

•**Whistles**- this seems to be a primary form of communication for dolphins. In bottle nosed dolphins each animal has their own unique whistle which is kind of like their name to other dolphins.

•**Bursts**- burst pulse sounds from dolphins are not as well understood but researchers have noted their frequency during aggressive behavior and as a way to maintain the social order of a pod.

Dolphin Breathing

Spinner-Dolphin-Takes-A-Breath

In order to breathe dolphins must make a trip to the surface and draw air in through the blow hole. This can be accomplished in a fraction of a second and when they exhale just before inhaling the air can move at an impressive 100 miles per hour. Once air has entered the blowhole it is quickly moved to the lungs and strong muscles close off the blowhole so the dolphin can dive. During their descent the air becomes pressurized and is absorbed in the lungs.

Dolphin Enemies and Threats

Most dolphins have few natural enemies. This makes them apex predators, or the top of the food chain.

A few smaller dolphin species are prey for larger sharks and even some wales but it is only the larger sharks that are a problem for the smallest of the species. Honestly the biggest threat to dolphin populations is humans.

One of the biggest problems for dolphins today is fishing nets. Commercial fishing operations use huge nets and drag the ocean for various types of fish. In the process they often snag dolphins or porpoises resulting in injury and death to thousands of animals every year.

In addition to accidental death from fishermen, dolphins are facing problems from pollution, especially the river varieties.

Playtime for Dolphins

Dancing-dolphins

A group of dolphins is known as a pod, and within the pod there is generally a lot of jumping and playing around. Though various reasons for jumping have been suggested, such as speedier travel and spotting food sources, researchers are not entirely sure why dolphins jump or play.

Dolphins-with-a-ball

Playtime can include making bubble rings and finding objects to toss around. They have even been known to harass other marine animals, apparently just for the fun of it.

Dolphin-Playing-With-A-Ball

A-Young-Dolphin-Playing

Common-bottlenose-dolphin-play

Baby Dolphin Facts

Mother-and-Baby-Dolphins

Baby dolphins are much bigger than human babies and depending on the species could weigh anywhere from 25 pounds to 300 pounds (killer whale babies).

Most dolphin species carry their babies for 12 months and will only have a baby once every 2-3 years. After birth baby dolphins, called calves, will nurse for about 12 months and may stay with mom up to 6 years learning how to hunt and care for themselves.

Only one other dolphin will be allowed around a new born baby dolphin and that is the "auntie". This female dolphin will assist the mother with caring, teaching and protecting the infant. Babies will often start eating fish, shrimp and crustaceans at about six months of age, though they may still nurse as well.

Dolphin-With-A-Baby-Floating-

Humans and Dolphins

Girl-and-dolphin

Humans and dolphins have a long history and people today find them just as fascinating as ever. It may be their friendly looking face or their natural intelligence, but whatever the reason people still want to see and interact with these funny creatures.

Around the world there are a number of dolphinariums, places where dolphins are kept in captivity so people have easier access to them. The most famous of these in the United States is Sea World. Similar to theme parks, visitors pay to view dolphins, watch trained dolphins perform and in some instances swim with the dolphins.

Happy-child-and-dolphins

Fun Facts about Dolphins

Dolphin brains are larger than human brains

•Dolphin flippers have five bones similar to the human hand

•Swimming and sleeping is common as only one side of the dolphin brain sleeps at one time

•Dolphins have been a part of the US military- trained to find underwater bombs

•Average dolphins can eat 33 pounds of fish per day- that is like a human eating 15 pounds of steak daily!

Printed in Great Britain
by Amazon